D1222173

Tiger Talk
People I Know

Friends

Leon Read

SEA-TO-SEA
Mankato Collingwood London

Contents

Look for Tiger on the pages of this book. Sometimes he is hiding.

Friends are people we like to be with.

Get together

Friends like doing
things together.

Some friends like bouncing around.

Some friends
like playing
together.

What do you do
with your friends?

Making friends

Making friends is easy. We can make friends wherever we go.

Don't be shy! Join in the fun!

gym club

6

I made friends on vacation.

church

play club

Where have you made friends?

7

Helping each other

Friends help each other in many ways.

They can help find things.

I've found my friend's dog.

They can
help you
dress up.

How do you help
your friends?

Tiger's friend

Tiger's friend is Rabbit.

Tiger likes Rabbit because:

Rabbit is funny.

Rabbit is fun to play with.

Rabbit eats carrots.

Tiger has made
a new friend.

Tiger is my
friend!

What do you like
about your friends?

Good friends

Some of
our friends
are good at...

playing sports...

...and climbing.

My friend Mark
is good at
making noise!

What things are your
friends good
at doing?

Sharing things

It is good to share things with friends.

We can
share food...

...and pens.

We can share books...

...and toys.

What do you share with your friends?

Arguing

Sometimes friends argue.

Michelle pushed me down.

Now Michelle feels sad.

When have you argued with your friends?

17

Making up

Friends make up when
they say sorry.

Sorry.

Michelle said sorry. We are friends again.

What can you do to show a friend you are sorry?

Birthday party

Sharon is going to her friend's birthday party.

She has an invitation from Alex.

Sharon has brought a present for Alex.

Alex shares his cake with his friends.

My invitations

Make party
invitations for
your friends. Use
luggage labels
and noisemakers.

1

2

Write down:

Your friend's name,
your name,
the party date,
place, and time.

Now decorate the label and tie it to a party blower.

③

④

Make more invitations and give them to your friends.

Word picture bank

Cake—P. 21

Arguing—P. 16

Invitation—P. 20, 22, 2?

Present—P. 21

Shy—P. 6

Sharing—P. 14, 21

This edition first published in 2010 by Sea-to-Sea Publications
Distributed by Black Rabbit Books
P.O. Box 3263, Mankato, Minnesota 56002
Copyright © Sea-to-Sea Publications 2010

Printed in USA
All rights reserved.

9 8 7 6 5 4 3 2

Published by arrangement with the Watts Publishing Group
Ltd, London.

Library of Congress Cataloging-in-Publication Data
Read, Leon.
  Friends / Leon Read.
      p. cm. -- (Tiger talk. People I know)
  Includes index.
  ISBN 978-1-59771-190-6 (hardcover)
  1. Friendship in children--Juvenile literature. 2. Friendship--Juvenile
literature. I. Title.
  BF723.F68R43 2010
  177'.62--dc22
                  2008048579

Series editor: Adrian Cole

Photographer: Andy Crawford (unless otherwise credited)

Design: Sphere Design Associates

Art director: Jonathan Hair
Picture researcher: Diana Morris
Consultants: Prue Goodwin and Karina Law

Acknowledgments:
The Publisher would like to thank Norrie Carr model agency.
"Tiger" and "Rabbit" puppets used with kind permission from
Ravensden PLC (www.ravensden.co.uk).
Tiger Talk logo drawn by
Kevin Hopgood.

There are 21 Tigers, including me, in this book.
Did you find all of us?